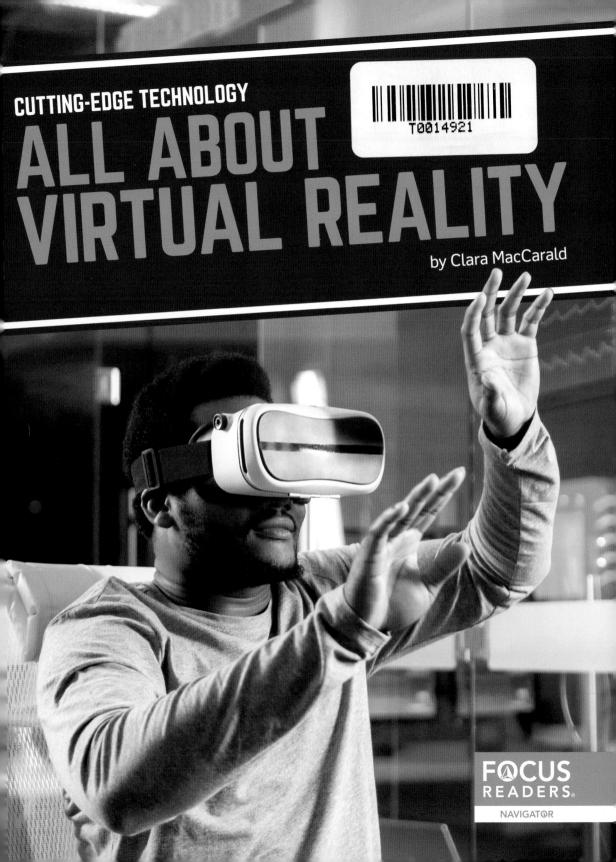

CUTTING-EDGE TECHNOLOGY

# ALL ABOUT VIRTUAL REALITY

by Clara MacCarald

T0014921

FOCUS READERS®

NAVIGATOR

# WWW.FOCUSREADERS.COM

Focus Readers is distributed by North Star Editions:
sales@northstareditions.com | 888-417-0195

Produced for Focus Readers by Red Line Editorial.

Content Consultant: Yuhao Zhu, PhD, Assistant Professor of Computer Science, University of Rochester

Photographs ©: Shutterstock Images, cover, 1, 4–5, 7, 8–9, 11, 19, 20, 22–23, 25; iStockphoto, 13, 15, 16–17, 26–27, 29

**Library of Congress Cataloging-in-Publication Data**
Library of Congress Cataloging-in-Publication Data is available on the Library of Congress website.

**ISBN**
978-1-63739-475-5 (hardcover)
978-1-63739-512-7 (paperback)
978-1-63739-582-0 (ebook pdf)
978-1-63739-549-3 (hosted ebook)

Printed in the United States of America
Mankato, MN
012023

## ABOUT THE AUTHOR

Clara MacCarald is a freelance writer who has written more than 40 nonfiction books for kids. She lives with her daughter and a small herd of cats in an off-grid house nestled in the forests of central New York.

# TABLE OF CONTENTS

# CHAPTER 1

# A VIRTUAL VISIT

You're sitting on the couch in your living room. You decide to go to the ocean. But you don't leave your house. Instead, you put on a **headset**. You move the lenses so they're in front of your eyes. Now it looks like you're underwater.

The ocean floor stretches out in front of you. Fish swim past. You turn your head

Virtual reality allows users to explore many places without leaving their homes.

from side to side. The water appears to be all around you. To the left, a sea turtle paddles by. A huge whale glides overhead. It makes a low grunting sound.

You are using virtual reality (VR). VR is an interactive **technology**. It puts users in a world created by a computer. VR worlds are three-dimensional (3D). That means they have height, width, and length. The computer allows users to see, hear, or touch parts of VR worlds. This interaction makes the worlds seem more real.

Some VR worlds are made-up. But VR can also create copies of real locations. It can show people cities on the other side of the world. Or it can make people

Some VR systems include treadmills that let users walk around virtual worlds.

feel like they're on another planet. VR can even re-create places or events from the past. The only limit is the inventors' imaginations.

# CHAPTER 2

# HOW VR WORKS

For most forms of VR, users wear headsets. Basic headsets attach to a smartphone. They fit around the phone and divide its screen in half. Other headsets are more complex. They have two displays, one for each eye. Some VR headsets connect to a computer with a cord. Other VR headsets are wireless.

Wireless headsets let users move freely. But they may run out of power and need to be charged.

Many VR headsets have headphones as well. That way, users can hear sounds in the virtual environment. Some headphones even block sounds from the real world.

Each VR headset shows two slightly different images. Together, they create a 3D effect. When the user turns her head, the headset tracks the movement with motion **sensors**. A computer changes the view to match. The user feels like she's looking in a different direction.

There are several kinds of motion sensors. Some use an outside device to watch the user and track the headset's position. Or there may be a camera on

Many VR controllers have buttons users can push to interact with the virtual world.

the headset. It looks around the room to determine if the headset is moving.

Sensors may also watch a user's body movement. The computer makes it seem as if the user is doing these actions in the VR world. Or, a user might hold hand controllers. As the user moves these controllers, the VR world responds. For example, controllers can let users grab objects. Or their motions may control settings or menus. Users can also wear VR gloves. The gloves stiffen to create the feeling of touching something.

Some VR systems use treadmills. These machines allow people to walk or

## AUGMENTED REALITY

Some systems use augmented reality (AR). Unlike with VR, AR users still see the real world. But a computer adds virtual bits. For example, a virtual monster might appear to run across an actual road. AR has practical uses, too. People can see how new clothes or furniture might look before buying them.

One augmented reality game has players find imaginary creatures in real-world locations.

run in place. Users can explore the VR world. Bars or belts might help keep users from falling.

Another kind of VR system doesn't use headsets. Instead, screens surround the user. The screens show the VR world. Even the floor may be part of the display.

# CREATING 3D

The brain uses both eyes to see in 3D. Each eye sees the world from a different angle. The brain compares the two images to figure out distances.

A close object, such as a hand in front of the face, seems to be in very different places to each eye. A faraway object looks almost the same in both eyes. A person's brain puts the two images together into one 3D image.

A VR headset copies the way people's eyes work. Each display shows a slightly different picture. The differences between the two pictures make objects appear closer to or farther from the VR user.

Headphones can add to the feeling of 3D. Like the eyes, the ears hear slightly different things. Sound reaches the closer ear first. Close sounds are also louder than distant sounds.

# HOW EYES SEE 3D

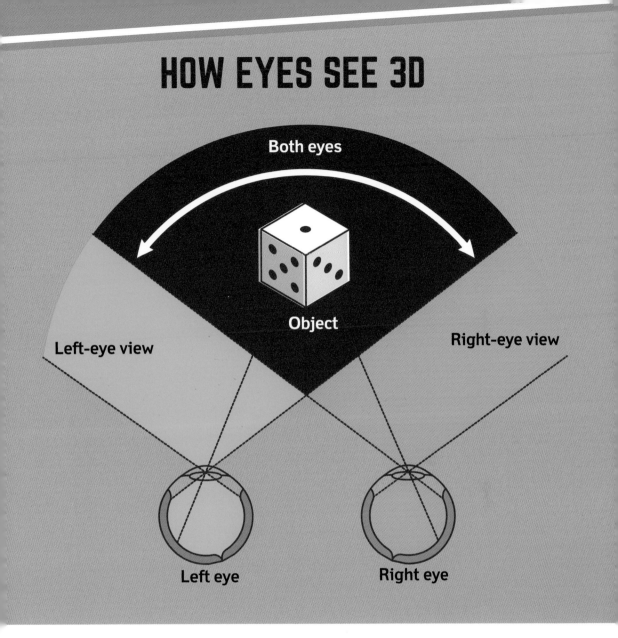

Both eyes

Object

Left-eye view

Right-eye view

Left eye

Right eye

VR uses these facts to make sounds and objects seem to move. It copies how people see and hear things in the real world.

# CHAPTER 3

# VIRTUAL WORLDS

People use virtual reality in many ways. Some VR worlds are made to entertain. For example, many video games use VR. Players might go on a quest or try to solve a mystery. They may talk to other characters or fight monsters. Or they may explore the game's map.

VR can make players feel and see the same things their characters do.

Games often have set characters for people to play. But sometimes each person has a unique **avatar**. Users can choose how their avatars look. And they can use their avatars to interact.

Avatars and VR are used outside of gaming, too. Some companies use VR worlds to hold meetings.

Many VR worlds help people learn. Students can visit famous places. They can safely see dangerous areas, such as volcanoes. Or they can go somewhere that's impossible to visit in real life, such as the inside of a **cell**.

People can also use VR for training. For example, soldiers can fight in practice

With VR, teachers can show students places that are too far away to visit on field trips.

battles. Pilots can learn to fly without leaving the ground. And medical students can build skills by caring for fake patients.

VR has other uses in health care, too. Surgeons can use VR to control robots during **operations**. VR can also help treat anxiety. Some people become too

At some museums and galleries, VR lets guests feel like they're going inside paintings.

anxious to do everyday activities, such as riding the bus. Practicing in VR can help people prepare to do these tasks in the real world.

VR can also benefit people who have difficulty moving. For instance, some people can't walk very far. They may feel stuck at home. VR offers them a way to travel.

In fact, VR worlds often copy physical spaces. People can visit **galleries** and museums in VR. Users might also watch a play or a movie.

People continue to plan and test new uses for VR. However, bringing these ideas to life takes time, money, and work.

# THE METAVERSE

Many companies have become interested in creating the metaverse. People disagree on exactly what the word *metaverse* means. But the general idea is an online VR space that's always open. Users could chat, play, have business meetings, and more. The metaverse might be one VR world. Or it might be many connected ones. People might even be able to buy virtual homes there.

# CHAPTER 4

# VR PROBLEMS

VR technology isn't perfect. Headsets can be large and uncomfortable. And if the VR view doesn't move quickly enough, users may experience **lag**. When that happens, the VR world feels less real. Some VR headsets are faster than others. But the fastest headsets often cost a lot of money.

Lag is a big problem in video games. It can make players lose or get frustrated.

Wearing a VR headset can give some people **motion sickness**. They may get headaches or feel dizzy. Some even throw up. Also, looking at any kind of screen for a long time can cause eye strain.

VR can cause accidents as well. When using VR systems, people cannot see the real world. They may trip, fall, or crash into things. Most accidents are small. But they can be serious. Some VR users have been badly hurt.

Critics worry that VR could affect users' behavior. People who use VR too much may have trouble relating to people in real life. Or they may try doing unsafe things. For example, they might jump or

It's important to follow safety instructions when using VR equipment. Otherwise, users may get hurt or feel sick.

climb in dangerous places because their avatars can do that in VR.

Kids in online VR worlds can encounter harmful content or people. Of course, the same thing can happen on regular websites. But VR makes everything feel more real. So, these dangers could have a bigger impact.

# CHAPTER 5

# THE FUTURE OF VR

In the early 2020s, more people than ever were interested in VR. In October 2021, the company Meta started a big push. It announced that it would spend $10 billion over the next year. The money would help develop VR technologies.

Companies were making cheaper and smaller headsets. Some headsets had

In 2022, VR headset prices ranged from less than $100 to more than $1,000.

new features. In 2022, Sony produced a headset that tracked the user's eye movement. The computer could then make an avatar's eyes move in VR. Sony was also working on a headset that reduced motion sickness.

Companies also made changes to better protect kids in VR worlds. For

## VIRTUAL SMELLS

In 2022, some inventors were working to add a new sense to the VR experience. One company created a device that went over the user's nose. The device let out a smell based on what the user did in the VR world. Smells came from chemicals mixed in a lab. Some smells were pleasant, like a rose. Other scents included garbage and dirt.

In the future, VR could use smaller devices, such as smart glasses.

example, Meta introduced new tools. The tools let parents see more of what their children were doing. All these updates aimed to make virtual reality safer and more fun.

# FOCUS ON
# VIRTUAL REALITY

*Write your answers on a separate piece of paper.*

1. Write a letter to a friend describing some of the problems related to VR.

2. What kind of VR world would you most like to experience? Why?

3. Which part of a VR headset tracks the user's movement?

    **A.** lenses
    **B.** sensors
    **C.** headphones

4. How would a VR headset make a noise seem farther away?

    **A.** The noise would sound quieter.
    **B.** The noise would sound louder.
    **C.** The noise would reach only one ear.

*Answer key on page 32.*

# GLOSSARY

**avatar**
A character that represents the user in a virtual world.

**cell**
The smallest unit of a living organism that can function and perform tasks.

**galleries**
Places where works of art, such as paintings, are shown.

**headset**
A device that goes on a user's head and covers the eyes.

**lag**
When sounds or images shown by a computer are too slow.

**motion sickness**
A feeling of being dizzy or unwell, caused by movement.

**operations**
Types of medical care in which doctors make cuts in the body to solve problems.

**sensors**
Devices that collect and report information.

**technology**
Machines and devices created using science.

# TO LEARN MORE

## BOOKS

Bodden, Valerie. *Virtual-Reality Headsets*. Minneapolis: Abdo Publishing, 2018.

Eboch, M. M. *The Future of Entertainment: From Movies to Virtual Reality*. North Mankato, MN: Capstone Press, 2020.

Peterson, Christy. *Cutting-Edge Virtual Reality*. Minneapolis: Lerner Publications, 2019.

## NOTE TO EDUCATORS

Visit **www.focusreaders.com** to find lesson plans, activities, links, and other resources related to this title.

# INDEX

**Answer Key:** 1. Answers will vary; 2. Answers will vary; 3. B; 4. A